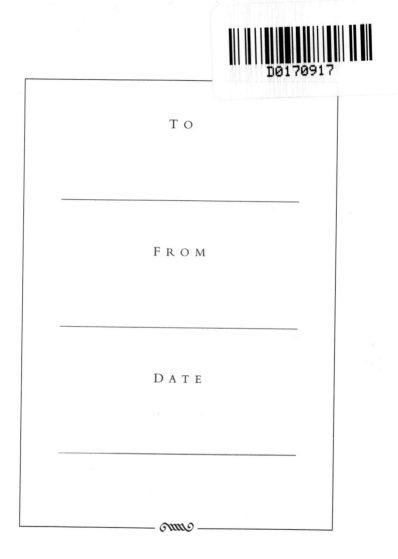

T O

_____

F R O M

_____

D A T E

_____

Thanks, Dad,

FOR TEACHING ME WELL

Thanks, Dad,

FOR TEACHING ME WELL

Ken Gire

WATERBROOK
PRESS

THANKS, DAD, FOR TEACHING ME WELL
PUBLISHED BY WATERBROOK PRESS
5446 North Academy Boulevard, Suite 200
Colorado Springs, Colorado 80918
A division of Random House, Inc.

Unless otherwise noted, all Scripture quotations are taken from
the New American Standard Bible® (NASB). © Copyright The
Lockman Foundation 1960, 1962, 1963, 1968, 1971, 1972, 1973,
1975, 1977, 1995. Used by permission. Scriptures marked (KJV)
are taken from the King James Version.

ISBN 1-57856-196-5

Copyright © 1999 by Ken Gire

Published in association with the literary agency of Alive
Communications, Inc., 1465 Kelly Johnson Blvd., Suite 320,
Colorado Springs, Colorado 80920

Gire, Ken.
    Thanks, Dad, for teaching me well / Ken Gire.—1st ed.
        p.   cm.
    ISBN 1-57856-196-5
    1. Father and child. 2. Fatherhood—Religious aspects—
Christianity. I. Title
HQ755.85.G57   1999
306.874'2—dc21   99-11157
                                                            CIP

Printed in the United States of America
1999—First Edition

10 9 8 7 6 5 4 3 2

I wish I could have told him
in the living years.

FROM THE SONG, "THE LIVING YEARS"
BY MIKE AND THE MECHANICS

Contents

Contents

Preface

WHEN YOU WERE A CHILD, he towered over you. In many ways, he still does.

He was the one you called on to kill the spider. The one you came to for the car keys. The one you counted on. For everything. For locking up the house at night to figuring out "some assembly required" Christmas morning. He showed you how to whistle, how to bait a hook, how to tie a tie. He taught you to pull a tooth and to parallel park. He footed the bill for most everything yet always found enough money for ice cream. He carried a picture of you in his billfold and kept a place for you in his heart. He had a name for you and a greeting for you. "Hey, tiger! How's m'boy?" or "Hi, sweetie! How's my little princess?"

Chances are, it was years before you learned he even had a name. The only one you knew him by was "Daddy."

Somewhere along the road to growing up, when the Ys began dropping off your friends' names, maybe the Y dropped off his name too, and he became simply "Dad."

The Y dropped off my daddy's name late in elementary school, shortly before his first heart attack. My junior-high, high-school, and college years were punctuated with emergency trips to the hospital, all-night vigils in waiting rooms, and slow periods of recovery at home. Through the years he underwent two open-heart surgeries, contracting hepatitis from a blood transfusion during one of them. Later in life he developed diabetes. Later still, cancer of the prostate.

Dad was a fighter, beating the odds against him by sometimes the narrowest of margins. But at age sixty-seven, the odds finally caught up with him.

He left behind no unfinished business, at least with me. He said most everything he needed to say. And I said most everything I needed to say.

There was one thing, though, I wish I had said more often. That one thing was "thanks."

Thanks for working so hard. For giving so much. And for never giving up. Thanks for taking me along and telling me stories. Thanks for teaching me so many values and for teaching them so well.

Thanks, Dad.

If your own father is still living, there is time to speak the words you have waited all of your life to say, and that he has waited all of his life to hear. Please don't wait.

Say them loud.

Say them clear.

Say them now.

In the living years.

CHAPTER ONE

Thanks for Teaching Me the Value of a Smile

The author's memories of his dad

MY DAD WAS A COACH in Texas during the years after World War II, a time when the country cinched its belt, rolled up its sleeves, and put a shoulder to the work of rebuilding everything from highways to high-school football programs. He took me to so many games, scouting other teams, that they all run together in a blur.

He took me fishing only once.

Maybe that is why I remember it so vividly.

It was summer, and we were staying in a small cabin in the mountains of Colorado. I don't remember where we were or how high we were. I remember only how cold it was and how wet. Shivering our way into the cabin after spending too much time outdoors, we pried off our shoes, peeled off our socks, and put them all on the rack inside the oven. We scooted our chairs in a half-circle and crowded around the open door of that oven. Our bare feet toeing the hot metal. Our numb fingers cradling cups of hot chocolate. Our cold noses warming to wisps of steam.

Before long, the smell of roasting leather filled the room. Now and then we pulled out a shoe to check if it was done. When it was, we squeezed a foot into its damp warmth. Then another foot. Ahhh, what a feeling.

On a morning of dry shoes and clear weather, my dad took me fishing. It was my first time on a lake, or in a boat, for that matter. I sat hunched up in the bow, while Dad sat tall in the stern. After lowering the anchor, he rigged up the rods and handed me mine. It was then I learned my first lesson about the sport: Fishing involves a lot of sitting.

Not being very good at that, I soon set aside my rod and tried my luck with the net, swishing it back and forth in the water with the boyish optimism that an unsuspecting lunker might just swim its way into it. While I was dredging the top twelve inches of the lake, a storm rolled in, causing the temperature to drop and the sky to darken. The water absorbed the darkness, turning the lake black and sinister. As the wind grew furious, slapping wave after wave against the boat, I steadied myself by clutching both sides of the bow.

Dad reeled in his line, pulled up the anchor, and yanked at the rope starter, once, twice, then again. The motor coughed to life. He opened the throttle and steered toward shore. The hull of the small wooden boat cut through the waves, sending sprays of water into the wind. The faster we went, the higher the bow lifted out of the water, and the harder it came crashing down. The spray felt as if someone were pelting my face with needles, a handful at a time.

I had never been so cold.

Or so scared.

In a boy's best effort at bravery, I clenched my teeth to keep them from chattering. I turned to see if Dad was all right. I will never forget the sight of his face jutted against the wind, his eyes riveted to the shore, his hand firm on the throttle. He glanced down at me, so miserably clumped in the bow, and seeing the fear in my eyes, he smiled. Through my chattering teeth, I smiled back. In that moment I knew. Everything would be all right. The boat would make it to shore. We would make it to the cabin. And we would be safe again, warm again, dry again, huddled around that open oven door.

I don't remember anything Dad said that day. Or anything I said. All I remember is that picture of him sitting in the stern of that boat and the peace that came over me when he smiled.

I have a sepia-tinted picture of him framed in my office. He is standing straight and tall in his army uniform. A soldier in his twenties. With wire-rimmed glasses. And that same smile.

It helped win the war, that smile. I'm certain of it. Not the whole war, of course, but the little wars along the way. The wars we fight within ourselves. To be brave in the cold, even though our teeth are chattering. To keep our eyes on the shore, regardless of the waves splashing over us. To stay the course, despite the winds galing against us. I'm certain that smile lifted the hopes of every soldier who saw it.

That smile also lifts *my* hopes every time I look at the picture. It makes me want to smile back. And to say thanks.

In the Lutheran church our family attended, the minister often ended his sermon with a benediction, praying that the Lord's face would shine on the congregation. Because I received the gift of my father's smile for so many years, I know the warmth a shining face brings to another person. And the peace. It's a peace that passes from a father to his son, and on its way, passes all understanding.

This much, though, I do understand.

Sometimes what you need most when you're going through a storm is a smile.

Especially a smile from someone you love.

Especially when that someone is your dad.

〰

The LORD bless you, and keep you;

The LORD make His face shine on you,

And be gracious to you;

The LORD lift up His countenance on you,

And give you peace.

NUMBERS 6:24-26

CHAPTER TWO

Thanks for Teaching Me the Value of Faith

Corrie ten Boom's memories of her dad, adapted from her book In My Father's House

I REMEMBER THE MORNING of my first day of school as if it were yesterday. There I was, this stubborn little Dutch girl. My hands wrapped around the railing of our stairs. My jaw set against the idea of leaving.

"I'm not going," I insisted. "I know how to read. I can learn arithmetic from Papa, and Caspernia needs me at home."

This stubborn little Dutch girl's will had triumphed.

Or so it seemed…until Papa walked across the room.

As he approached, I braced myself for the confrontation, clutching the railing even tighter. Then, with such tenderness in his voice, he said, "Of course you're not going to school alone, Corrie. I am going to walk with you."

Papa bent down, his long beard brushing against my head, and one by one he loosened my fingers. With each one he pried loose, the louder I protested. But his large, strong hands won out over the protests, and I found my hand gripped in his. I tried to twist free, but the harder I pulled, the tighter he gripped.

I went with him out the door, but I went kicking and screaming. If he was going to make me go to school, I was going to make the whole neighborhood aware of it. I struggled energetically every inch of the way, red-faced and furious.

Papa, in contrast, conducted himself with great dignity. He didn't yell or scream or once threaten me. He simply pulled me along behind him by the sheer, irresistible force of his will. What a sight we were. Him, walking tall and proper in his crisp, clean suit. Me, twisting and turning and telling the whole neighborhood what an injustice was happening in its streets.

When we finally reached the school, I saw one father carrying his boy into the classroom, his arms and legs flailing, his lungs bellowing. Fearing I looked just as silly, I immediately stopped resisting.

As soon as I did, Papa released my hand, which suddenly throbbed back to life. He bent over again, this time to kiss my cheek. In his own kind and reassuring way, he told me that when school was over, he would be waiting for me at home. And that was all I needed to know to get me through that first, fearful day of school.

Sixty-seven years later, the memory of that day came back to me.

After the war, some friends and I founded a house in Holland for concentration-camp survivors, which we later expanded to be a respite for any who were simply weary and needing rest. The rooms were large and luxurious, and I had grown to love how comfortable and familiar they were. After traveling a great deal, staying in unfamiliar rooms, sleeping in strange beds, and socializing with strangers, I settled in a room of my own. The room was filled with my furniture, as was most of the house. On the wall were photographs of those I loved.

I held on to every picture, every piece of furniture, every reminder of the happy times our family had shared before the war. I held on to them the same way I had held on to the railing of our stairs as a young girl resisting the long and frightful walk to school.

I left the house temporarily to fulfill some speaking commitments. Weeks later when I came back, someone had taken the pictures off the wall of my room and placed their personal belongings on my bed. I couldn't believe it. I had not told my friends of my decision to return to this room; still, had they not known how much staying there meant to me, how much I loved the house, my room, my things? I knew they needed the room for the people they were caring for, but what about me? What about my care? Where would I go?

Over the clamor of those voices came the calm voice of my heavenly Father. "Only obey Me, Corrie. I'll hold your hand. It is My will that you leave your room. Later you will thank Me for this experience. You do not see it, but this is one of My great blessings for you."

I packed my bags and said good-bye to my friends and to the cozy familiarity of that house. Where was

God leading me? To the green pastures and quiet waters of America. As promised, He held my hand every step of the way. And as promised, it was a great blessing. I traveled across the United States, speaking and giving my testimony. The meetings grew in size. The response was overwhelming. People began to experience the love of God, accepting not only His forgiveness but passing it on to others who had hurt them and wronged them in the past.

Seeing all the blessings I experienced in America, I was thankful for my heavenly Father's hands. Hands that were stronger than mine. Hands that taught me to let go and let Him lead. Hands I first came to trust when Papa took my hand in his and led me to that first day of school.

☙

The LORD is my shepherd,

I shall not want.

He makes me lie down in green pastures;

He leads me beside quiet waters.

He restores my soul;

He guides me in the paths of righteousness

For His name's sake.

Even though I walk through the valley of the

shadow of death,

I fear no evil, for You are with me.

PSALM 23:1-4

CHAPTER THREE

Thanks for Teaching Me the Value of God

Larry Crabb's memories of his dad, adapted from the book he coauthored with his dad, God of My Father

FOR MANY PEOPLE the word *father* connotes bad memories. In their emotional thesaurus it means one who abandons, abuses, demeans, and demands perfection. Small wonder that fathers all too often represent obstacles, not avenues, to embracing the concept of God as Father.

For me the word *father* brings to mind the *best* of memories. For me it is an avenue, for I have been drawn to love God by my father.

My father's story covers not only a span of years but of emotions. He grew up on Germantown Avenue in Philadelphia in the early 1900s. With a family of six he lived in a second-story apartment above the Germantown Gospel Hall, where they all worshiped.

In 1917, when my dad was only five, his father wired the Gospel Hall with electricity, determined to have the job completed in time for Sunday morning worship. Grandpa worked steadily on the project from Monday after dinner until Wednesday night, when he paused for the weekly prayer meeting. He continued his work the next day and pressed forward on into the weekend. The last two nights he worked he had a high fever, but he kept going by wrapping cold cloths around his head. By Sunday morning the lights were working, but he couldn't go to the service to see them. He was in bed with the flu.

He stayed in bed all the next week. In spite of the doctor's coming to care for him, he got worse. My dad helped Grandma take care of his father, but by now Grandpa was delirious with fever, tossing and turning, his bedclothes wet with perspiration. In a moment of lucidity, Grandpa looked at my then five-year-old father, and, with tenderness in his eyes, put his arms around him. He uttered the words, "Don't cry. *Hush, God is in it.*"

And he died.

My grandpa's death was a devastating experience for my dad. It also left my grandma alone to finish raising the family. But she never felt alone. She had her children, who were not only a source of delight but of support. When my dad was only seven, he worked with his nine-year-old brother after school in a fruit store. When they weren't needed at the store, they sold brushes and mops door-to-door.

They gladly gave their mother their hard-earned income, for which she was always thankful. "Children," she would say, "you see how God has provided this extra income just in the nick of time." Always conscious of God's care, she often quoted Psalm 68:5 from her King James Bible: "A father of the fatherless, and a judge of the widows, is God in his holy habitation." Then she would point out the verse. "There it is, children. God said it."

It was she who taught my dad not only about the wonderful promises of the Bible, but about the wonderful God who had made those promises. She taught her children how to pray to this God, not so much corporately as individually and personally.

Each night my dad knelt beside his bed and prayed something like this: "Heavenly Father, Thou hast taken Papa to be with Thyself, and in Thy holy Word Thou hast promised to take care of my mother, brother, sisters, and myself. When I say or do anything to grieve Thee, may I quickly confess to Thee and so keep happy and smiling for Thee. Amen."

Today we look upon the *thees* and *thous* of the King's English with a certain amused condescension. My dad looked upon them with innocent reverence. When he prayed, he had the posture of a child kneeling before majesty, a majesty that was compatible with intimacy but never obscured by it.

His prayers, which came from a heart that had been broken at an early age, taught me the meaning of the word *transcendent*. His prayers taught me that beyond my life there exists a story that is bigger than mine. I grasped something of that bigger story when I was only four years old. Even after all the years that have passed, the memory is still clear.

It was a Sunday morning. About fifty people had gathered in a circle around a table to partake in the Lord's Supper. In the middle of the table, covered with a white cloth, were the elements. I was lying on the floor. As my dad stood to pray, I looked up at him.

And as I listened to him pray, I thought, *He actually thinks he's talking to someone. And whoever it is means more to him than anyone else does.*

The greatest gift my parents gave me was the realization that I was not the most important person in their lives. Neither was my brother. Neither were they to each other. Not even the family was more important to them than God.

As odd as seventeenth-century English sounded to the ear of a four-year-old, this much I understood, although it was years before I could articulate it: Everyone's life is a story whose point is discovered only when that story is lifted up into the larger story of God. We're not the point; none of us. God is. There is a story bigger than ours, a story that transcends every other.

And until we see our story as only a subplot in that eternal drama, we'll never see the meaning. I learned that lesson from my father.

He went forward a little, and fell on the ground,
and prayed that, if it were possible,
the hour might pass from him.
And he said, "Abba, Father,
all things are possible unto thee;
take away this cup from me:
nevertheless not what I will, but what thou wilt."

MARK 14:35-36 (KJV)

CHAPTER FOUR

Thanks for Teaching Me the Value of Sharing My Faith

Patty Threlkeld Dorn's memories of her dad,
as told to the author

I GREW UP A SOUTHERN GIRL. Southern girls who adore their fathers often refer to them fondly as "Daddy" their entire lives.

Daddy loved to fish. And he loved taking me with him. As a young girl, I would sit at home, fidgeting for him to return from work. When his car turned into the driveway, I shot out the front door to greet him, where he swept me into his loving arms. After changing into his fishing clothes, he gathered our gear, and we drove to the docks.

The docks. I still remember the sound of them, weathered and creaky, under my little feet as we walked over the planks, holding hands and fishing rods. And the air. I can smell it today if I just close my eyes. Tangy with salt. A hint of fish. The allure of faraway adventure.

Somewhere along the edge of the dock we would park ourselves, our feet dangling off the edge. And while Daddy baited our hooks, he would ask me about my day. As our little corks bobbed on the water, he listened. Sometimes we caught fish, sometimes not. And sometimes Daddy didn't fish at all. He just helped me with my pole and sat next to me, talking, listening, basking in the moment we shared together on that dock.

It was then I realized.

It wasn't the fishing that was important to him.

It was me.

He just wanted to be with me.

How could a daughter not adore a daddy like that, even if she weren't southern?

On the days we got up early to fish, Daddy took me to breakfast. We'd stop at some little restaurant, always ordering the same thing. Biscuits and gravy. Oh, how he loved to sop up that gravy with those biscuits. I loved those fluffy biscuits too. And that gravy. Mm-mm.

But maybe I would have loved whatever he ordered— scrambled eggs, oatmeal, pancakes, whatever. Maybe it wasn't the food at all. Maybe it was just being together, him and me, sitting at that booth, me feeling so grown-up and so special.

After a final cup of coffee, he would wipe his mouth with a napkin, pay the waitress, and we were off to the docks.

Daddy always made me feel that being with me was a special event in his day. He still makes me feel that way. Every time I see him, his face lights up, he hugs me, and he tells me how wonderful it is to see me.

He still takes me fishing.

It's in his blood. He's been doing it since the time he could walk and knows more about the sport than anyone I know. No matter what lake we fish, he almost always outfishes everyone there. That's because he can "read" a lake and knows, almost instinctively, where the fish are and what they're feeding on. He hauls 'em in when no one else is getting even a nibble.

And here's what invariably results.

Before long, a nearby fisherman reels in his line, makes his way over to where Daddy is, and starts asking him questions. I am usually fishing a few yards away in a spot of my own, all the while watching and listening.

Daddy greets the man with that warm, embracing smile of his and shows him the flies he has personally tied and the plastic bubble that goes with them. As the man admires the rig, Daddy asks, "Would you like me to set your line up like mine?"

The reply almost always is "Sure!" or "That'd be great," or "If it's not too much trouble."

The man offers to pay Daddy, but he just shoos off the suggestion. He rigs up the man's line, then does something extraordinary. (You would have to be a fisherman to know just how extraordinary.) He offers the man his fishing spot.

"Come stand right here. There, that's it. Now cast over there. Good."

The man is really smiling now, suddenly a kid again. The adult in him, though, again offers money. But again, Daddy declines it.

"One thing I would like, though," Daddy says.

"What's that?"

"A few minutes of your time."

And as the man fishes, Daddy tells him about the Father's love, a love so great that He sent His Son not only to tell us about His love, but to demonstrate it by dying for our sins. After Daddy finishes explaining the gospel, he asks if the man wants to invite Christ into his life. Often the answer is yes, and the man stops fishing and prays.

Then Daddy turns and waves me over. "Patty, I want you to meet so and so. He just became a believer!" And we all celebrate. Then Daddy lets the person get back to his fishing, all the while sharing with him how to grow in Christ by reading the Bible, telling him how to get started. After the fish are caught and the person calls it a day, Daddy and I talk about what has just happened and pray for the person.

Daddy has taught me a valuable lesson on those fishing trips. He tells the same story but always tailors it to the person he is talking to. "Jesus didn't share the gospel the same way twice," Daddy would tell me. "It's important to listen to people, and to meet them where they are."

Seeing him share Christ with literally hundreds of people over the years, I have gained a heart to share Christ with others too. I have also developed a fisherman's skill at doing it.

He is a fisherman and a fisher of men.

I am a southern girl and his daughter.

I still call him Daddy.

And I still adore him. Now more than ever.

ℂℳℬℯ

Now as Jesus was walking by the Sea of Galilee,

He saw two brothers, Simon who was called Peter,

and Andrew his brother,

casting a net into the sea;

for they were fishermen.

And He said to them,

"Follow Me, and I will make you fishers of men."

MATTHEW 4:18-19

CHAPTER FIVE

Thanks for Teaching Me the Value of My Name

The author's memories of his dad

MY BIRTH CERTIFICATE READS: "Kenneth Paxton Gire II."

Pretty impressive name tag for a seven-pounder.

It was my dad's name. Technically I was a "junior," but my mother never liked the sound of that, so she put the "II" after my name.

When I was old enough to learn it, I thought it was kind of special. Especially when I started school, because one of the first things you learn is how to write your name.

"Kenneth Paxton Gire II."

It looked distinguished, I thought, as I sat back and admired it in its entirety.

And when I pronounced it, it had a certain "royal lineage" ring to it, as if there might have been a king or a prince of something somewhere in my background.

As I grew older, though, the ring started getting on my nerves, mainly because I found myself always having to explain it. Here's how the conversations would go when someone learned I was named after my dad.

"So, you're a junior?"

To which I would answer, "No, I'm 'the second.'" And the person would look at me quizzically. In that awkward moment, I felt compelled to fill the silence with something. "That's the way it is on the birth certificate," I would say, my voice dropping in confidence over the years, and my words sounding less like an explanation and more like an apology.

Most let it go at that. One or two would correct me. "It's 'junior' if you're named after your father. It's 'the second' if you're named after your grandfather."

How would a kid know that? I'm an adult, and I'm not even sure it's true.

So what's a kid to do, except come clean? "My mom. She did it. She's the one who made 'em write it that way."

Dad and I were innocent of any genealogical wrongdoing.

When friends first started calling me on the phone—sometime late in elementary school—that created another problem. When they asked, "Is Ken there?" my mom would reply, "Do you want to speak to Big Ken or Little Ken?"

That was okay when I was in elementary school.

Once I got to junior high, though...

"Hey, *Little Ken*," some guy would say, snickering as he passed in the hall.

Just what a junior-high kid needs. More humiliation.

The "II" followed me through life. After a while, I got tired of the explaining and started signing my name simply, "Ken Gire, Jr." And after Dad died in 1986, I dropped the "Jr."

Over the years I occasionally ran into people who knew my dad. Since he had been a coach, a teacher, and later an administrator in the public school system, a lot of people knew him.

When I said my name or wrote it on a job application or some other form, I might hear these words: "Gire? You're not *Kenneth* Gire's boy, are you?" or "Are you related to *Coach* Gire?"

"He's my dad."

And the person would break into a smile and launch off on a story.

"I had him as a teacher, at Paschal. He really made world history interesting."

"He was a great coach, really knew the game."

"He got me a job when I was unemployed."

"Oh boy, did your dad ever ride herd on me. But he kept me from quittin' school. He did, sure enough."

Through the snippets of stories I heard over the years, I was able to fashion a more complete picture of my dad. I knew him only as a son. Not as someone he coached or taught or worked with.

One morning when I was older, I was supposed to substitute teach for a Sunday school class at a downtown church, and I was running late. As I was speeding down the freeway, trying to make up time, I heard a siren. I looked in my rearview mirror and saw the flashing lights of a police car. I pulled off the freeway, and the policeman asked for my driver's license. In my hurry to get to church, I had left it at home. As I was explaining all this to the officer, he took out his ticket book. My eye fell on my Bible in the front seat, which had my name lettered on the front cover. I handed it to him. "This is the only identification I have."

He read the name and smiled. "You *Coach* Gire's boy?"

"He's my dad."

"I played for him at North Side High School. He was a great coach, your daddy."

"I never had him as a coach…but he's a great dad."

"I bet he is. Tell him hello for me, will ya? The name's Chadwell. Jimmy Chadwell. He'll remember." He smiled and said, "Keep an eye on the speed." And he said goodbye and let me go.

My dad once told me that a name isn't a label to distinguish you from the next guy. "It's who you are," he explained. "And who you are follows you all your life. You're a Gire, Son. That's special. That means something. And you've got to live in such a way to make sure it continues to mean something."

In my life the name Gire became slowly eclipsed by the name Christian. A greater name. A more glorious name. A name derived from a King.

So I do come from a royal lineage. Who would have thought?

I feel privileged to bear both names. I deserve neither. Both were given to me. As gifts. One through the love of my parents. The other through the love of God.

I'm a Gire, named after my dad.

And I'm a Christian, named after Christ.

Both names mean something.

I don't always live up to either.

But I know that both are worth living up to.

And thanks to my dad, I am trying.

ᏎᎯᏇ

A good name is to be more desired than great wealth.

PROVERBS 22:1

CHAPTER SIX

Thanks for Teaching Me
the Value of Me

Bart Campolo's memories of his dad, adapted
from the book he coauthored with his dad,
Things We Wish We Had Said

MY DAD IS TONY CAMPOLO. An incredibly tough act
to follow. Strong Christian leader. Dynamic speaker.
Passionate college professor. Best-selling author. Successful
in every sense of the word.

But of all the things he's succeeded at, this one thing
has meant the most to me: While I was a boy, he succeeded
at making me believe that I was the most essentially

wonderful person he had ever laid eyes on. That, more than anything else, has made the difference in my life.

Some people think parenthood is about setting a good example. That's partly true. Some think parenthood is about instilling the right principles. That's partly true too. Some think parenthood is about developing discipline. And that's partly true as well. But when everything is said and done, I think parenthood is about creating an indestructible sense of personal worth that the child will need to draw on for the rest of his life.

Everybody fails at something at some time in life. Everybody gets discouraged. Everybody at one time or another wants to give up. How we face the obstacles in our lives depends heavily on how we see ourselves. And how we see ourselves has a lot to do with the image of ourselves we see reflected in the people around us, especially as we are growing up.

My dad was the first person who taught me that, back when I was just a nine-year-old kid sitting in on his sociology class at the University of Pennsylvania. He was explaining Charles Cooley's theory of the Looking-Glass Self, the theory that how a person sees himself is largely determined by how he thinks the most important people in his world see him. Cooley termed these individuals "significant others."

I understood the concept, even as a nine-year-old. What I didn't understand was that I was looking at and listening to *my* most significant other. My dad.

Even when I failed once at a job, he told me how proud he was of me and that I could come home and work for him, because he always needed a person like me. I know I am infinitely precious because for as long as I can remember I have been infinitely precious to my dad.

I was always his highest priority. Over and over again, he said things and did things that made me certain I was more important than his friends, his work, his money, his possessions, even more important than himself. He did this in little ways. Little offhand comments that let me know how much I meant to him. Casually made decisions that let me know how much I mattered.

Like the day we drove together to a church where he was going to preach. As we drove, he told me he would rather be with me than any of his adult friends because I was more fun to be with.

After the church service, he and I were going to see an automobile race. It was the Langhorne 150, where Bobby Unser won the Bardahl Special after Mario Andretti's STP Racer got a flat tire with only twenty laps to go. That whole day was magical to me. Not because of the spectacle of the racetrack. Not because of the fame of the drivers. Not even because of the thrill of the race. The day was magical because I was sitting next to someone who thought I was more fun to be with than any of his friends.

Years later I got my driver's license and proceeded to drive as if I were racing in the Langhorne 150 myself. I had five accidents in three months. Although Dad felt he had to take my license away because I was such a threat on the road, he never said anything about the cars. What he did say I'll never forget.

"Cars can be replaced—you can't."

The last accident I had was a bad one. I came home frightened and embarrassed and dazed. What did he do? He took me out to shoot baskets. I got the message. So what if I couldn't drive—I was still okay with him.

I'm sure my dad looks back on my childhood and remembers milestone events, like family vacations, first date, graduation. I remember other things. Like the time he flew back from Chicago and drove straight to the soccer field to see one of my high-school games, then flew right back to Chicago to finish his work. He missed a night's sleep because he knew how much his presence at that soccer game meant to me. I remember things like that because they convinced me that I counted for something.

Things like the day he checked me out of school for a "family emergency."

I was called out of class to the principal's office, more than a little worried about what the emergency might be. Some emergency. Dad took me to lunch at a deli, then to an afternoon movie, which I liked so much that we sat through the second showing. I'll never forget that day. Or what he said to me: "School is never as important as you are."

Moments like that made such an indelible impression because I knew the sacrifices my dad had made to be with me were all expressions of his love.

For me the gospel was a natural extension of a love I had experienced all my life. It told me what my dad had told me all along. That I had value. And that I was worth a few sacrifices.

෧ᴎᴎᴑ

For God so loved the world,
that He gave His only begotten Son....

JOHN 3:16

CHAPTER SEVEN

Thanks for Teaching Me the Value of Tenderness

Linda Glasford's memories of her dad,
as told to the author

MY DAD WORKED more than twenty years as a policeman, keeping the peace in Peoria, Illinois.

He is a barrel-chested man, six feet tall, and a rugged outdoorsman. As a child, I always felt safe when I was around him. It didn't matter when it was, day or night, sunshine or storm. And it didn't matter where we were, cruising around in the family car in the center of town or fishing from his boat in the middle of a lake.

He was constantly teaching me things as a young girl, even from that boat. One specific piece of wisdom he continually shared with me, especially when something worried me, whether it was a storm in the middle of that lake or one in the middle of a grade-school friendship. "The Lord is still on the throne," he would say. And then he would pray with me, and suddenly the world was bright again and beautiful again.

Often he would bring sunshine into my world by picking me up at lunchtime and taking me to see the road crew building the interstate. Invariably, he would see something and point it out to me—a bug, for example—and he would somehow find a lesson in it. Or if the season was changing, he'd have something to teach me about that, and how it applied to my growing up or to his growing old.

He particularly was persistent in teaching me a lesson

about money. He was generous, and I was an only child. What a combination. So many times as a young girl I would hit him up for money. We're not talking nickels and dimes. We're talking a dollar a shot, which was a lot of money back then for a young girl to have burning a hole in her pocket.

I would ask, "Daddy, do you have a dollar?"

And he would say, "Linda, what happened to the dollar I gave you yesterday?"

"I spent it," I'd say, without a tinge of regret.

Then he would take out his wallet and pull out a bill. But before he handed it to me, he would say, "The reason Daddy has a dollar is because Daddy didn't spend a dollar."

Because I was always asking for money, this developed into a running dialogue that lasted throughout my childhood.

"Daddy, do you have a dollar?"

"What happened to the dollar I gave you yesterday?"

"I spent it."

And surrendering still another dollar, he'd add, "The reason Daddy has a dollar is because Daddy didn't spend a dollar."

As a child, I thought that as long as I spent the dollar and he didn't, we had a pretty good thing going. As I grew older, I realized he was trying to teach me his frugality. What I learned from him, though, was his generosity.

Although Dad was constantly teaching me things, the lessons that meant the most to me were things he wasn't even aware he was teaching. His sense of humor, for example.

He was fun to be with, always quick with a smile and always able to make me laugh. From all those happy moments together he taught me what a joy I was to him. Only God knows what effect that had on shaping me into the person I am today.

Dad taught me how to treat others, though he probably didn't realize it at the time. He knew everyone in town, and he would talk with everyone. It didn't make any difference whether the person was the head cardiologist at the hospital or the garbage collector on the poor side of town. Dad always treated everyone with dignity and respect. Even the people he arrested. And the day after the arrest, he would visit the person in jail to share Christ with him.

Those pictures of him have taught me so much.

So have the pictures that reveal his tenderness.

Dad's tenderness is not only what I remember most about him, it is what I treasure most. He was that way with me, with other people, even with animals.

He would stop for any injured animal he came across, bring it home, and nurse it back to health. It didn't matter what it was. I remember his being called to a fire where he was one of the first squad cars on the scene. Finding a baby bunny that was hurt, he put it in his coat, brought it home, and took care of it until it recovered. Once some baby birds fell through our chimney, and he took care of them, too. He fed them with a little bottle and later hand-fed them until they were big enough and strong enough to fly away.

He was that way with anything that was hurt, or anybody.

I remember a time on a cold, windy day after we had eaten at a small, out-of-town restaurant. We were taking a country road to get home when Dad saw a man lying on the roadside, signaling with a cigarette lighter. Dad pulled over to help. The man had just crashed his small airplane in a cornfield and had lost a lot of blood from a compound fracture in his leg. Another car stopped, then left to call an ambulance. Dad stayed with the man, got some cardboard out of his trunk to shield him from the wind, and a blanket to keep him from the cold. He stayed right beside the man in the subfreezing weather until the paramedics arrived and took him to the hospital. The next day, my dad visited him there, and the doctor said that ten more minutes in the cold and the man would have died of exposure. My dad then shared the gospel with the injured pilot.

That was my dad. That was who he was underneath the uniform.

Dad always treated me with tenderness, too. Even when he disciplined me. When I was two or three years old, I wandered off the porch into the yard, which had no fence and bordered a well-trafficked street. Dad ran to catch me, brought me inside, and told me he had to give me a spanking.

Stunned, I looked up at him and said, "Daddy, don't you love Linda anymore?"

He looked down at me and answered, "It's because I love you that I'm spanking you."

When he finished spanking me, I looked up at him again. This time, tears were streaming down his face.

I will always remember the tears he shed…and the birds he fed.

I will always remember the dollars he gave…and the life he saved.

I will always remember the gun he carried in his belt and the Bible he carried in his squad car.

The one revealed the way he made his living.

The other, the way he lived his life.

His name is Bill. He's retired now. But he's still on duty as my dad. Still my best friend. And still and forever my hero.

∽∾

Blessed are the poor in spirit,
for theirs is the kingdom of heaven.
Blessed are those who mourn, for they shall be comforted.
Blessed are the gentle, for they shall inherit the earth.
Blessed are those who hunger and thirst for righteousness,
for they shall be satisfied.
Blessed are the merciful, for they shall receive mercy.
Blessed are the pure in heart, for they shall see God.
Blessed are the peacemakers,
for they shall be called sons of God.

MATTHEW 5:3-9

CHAPTER EIGHT

Thanks for Teaching Me the Value of Humility

Senator John Ashcroft's memories of his dad, adapted from his book Lessons from a Father to His Son

THIS PICTURE OF MY FATHER that I'm about to share with you was taken in the autumn of his life. Late autumn. The changing colors of autumn's leaves, just before they fall, are a highlight of the season. From a chemical perspective, here is how the change takes place. As the hours of sunlight grow shorter, the trees produce less green chlorophyll. When the green of this natural chemical departs from the trees, the leaves are finally able to reveal the true glory of their natural colors.

Much like a mighty tree, my dad's true colors were the most vivid at the end of his life. It was an experience I will never forget.

The night before I was sworn into the Senate in 1995, my father gathered a small group of close friends and family for dinner. Seeing a piano in the corner of the room, my father said, "John, why don't you play the piano and we'll sing."

"Okay, Dad. You name it. I'll play it."

"Let's sing, 'We Are Standing on Holy Ground.'"

It was one of his favorites.

After the song, I eased away from the piano keys, and, thinking out loud, I said, "We're standing here having a good time, but I really wish we were in a dedication service." (Before each of my inaugurations as governor, friends would gather for such a service at my request, and we would invite God to be present in both the inaugural festivities and my administration.)

My lifelong friend Dick Foth spoke up. "We can do something about a dedication service, John."

At his suggestion, we gathered the next morning at a house not far from the Capitol, a beautiful house maintained by a group of friends for the express purpose of bringing members of Congress together for spiritual enrichment.

We began by chatting informally, then sang a hymn or two. At the time I didn't know just how weak my father was. He had been losing weight through the months of November and December and had told an acquaintance of his, "I'm hanging on by a thread, and it's a thin thread at that, but I'm going to see John sworn into the Senate."

As we talked, the earnestness of my father's voice

suddenly commanded everyone's attention. "John," Dad said, "please listen carefully." My children and I fixed our eyes on him. My brother Bob moved to the edge of his seat. Dick Foth and the others leaned in.

"The spirit of Washington is arrogance," my dad said, "and the spirit of Christ is humility. Put on the spirit of Christ. Nothing of lasting value has ever been accomplished in arrogance."

Suddenly the room went quiet. There was no chit-chat, no lighthearted banter, no whispering even. It was a profound moment. And everyone there knew it.

For a while we discussed my father's words. After that, I asked for prayer.

I knelt in front of the sofa where my father was seated. Everyone gathered around me to place a hand on my head or my shoulder or my back. Everyone was standing when I noticed my father lunging and swinging his arms as he tried to lift himself out of the overstuffed sofa. With a damaged heart operating at less than one-third capacity, he was expending every bit of energy he had, but he wasn't making much progress.

I felt terrible. Knowing he didn't have the strength, I said, "Dad, you don't have to struggle to stand and pray over me with these friends."

"John," my father answered, *"I'm not struggling to stand; I'm struggling to kneel."*

Some statements are so profound that they take awhile to sink in; others hit you with the force of a nuclear explosion. I thought my father's words might vaporize me on the spot.

Those words took me back to those early mornings as a child when I joined him on his knees, praying that we would do noble things. Now, still on his knees, he was taking me there again.

On the night after my swearing-in ceremony as a senator, my wife and I were awakened by a rattling of the iron bars outside our Washington apartment. It was my friend Dick Foth. He told me of my father's death. Then he told me this:

"Yesterday, your father pulled me aside and said, 'Dick, I want you to assure me that when John gets to his assigned offices, you will have prayer with him, inviting the presence of God into those rooms.'

"I looked at your father and said, 'We'll do just that. And, as a matter of fact, we'll call you up in Springfield, put you on the speaker phone, and you can join us for the consecration.'

"Your father grabbed me by the arm and said, 'You don't understand. I'll be with you, but I won't be in Springfield.'

"He knew what was coming, John. He knew."

My dad had little energy left those last days of his life. And he chose to spend it passing on to me his deepest understanding of life. His heart made one final and valiant effort, then he was gone.

Good-bye, Dad.

Thanks for the lessons.

And thanks for struggling to kneel.

I'm still struggling to learn.

౧౧౧౦

Clothe yourselves with humility toward one another,
for God is opposed to the proud,
but gives grace to the humble.

1 PETER 5:5

CHAPTER NINE

Thanks for Teaching Me the Value of Stories

The author's memories of his dad

THE TRANSITION BETWEEN MY CHILDHOOD and my adolescence came abruptly. It arrived suddenly one day late in my elementary-school years when my dad suffered a near-fatal heart attack. For six weeks he lay in intensive care, teetering between life and death, hooked up to tubes and IVs and monitoring devices.

Like a sudden but devastating earthquake, that event shook our home to its foundation. We had grown up praying mostly in liturgical ways, repeating set prayers

out loud, certain ones for church, for dinner, for bed-
time. In a moment, all that changed. We prayed personally now—and desperately. We prayed privately and
together. Others prayed with us, for us. They brought
food and baby-sat and helped in ways that I as a child
could never have imagined.

Little by little Dad got better and stronger, and the
day came when the hospital finally let him come home.

The jolt of that experience changed our lives. In many
ways, the changes were forever.

Some of the changes in my dad were spiritual. Others
were physical. He stopped smoking, for one. He started
watching his diet, eating things like tuna fish rinsed of
its oil under the kitchen faucet, salads, dry toast. And he
started exercising. He walked, because walking was all
he could do. He walked at night, because so many Texas
days are dripping with heat and humidity. He did it

religiously, every night after supper. Often he would ask if I wanted to go along. And most often I did.

We walked for blocks and blocks and blocks. Down the lamplit streets of our neighborhood. Into foreign neighborhoods. Past street names I had never heard of. Past houses I had never seen. When we completed the circuit, he'd sometimes ask, "How about one more time?" And we'd do it all over again. We walked so long that when I finally got home and took my shoes off, my feet throbbed. Sometimes I soaked them in cool water to put out the heat they radiated.

As we walked, I tried to keep up with his stride, no easy thing for a young boy with shorter legs. I tried to keep up mainly because he told me once while we were walking that buddies always walked in step with each other. I never forgot that. And I never stopped trying to stretch my stride to match his. When I did, it was such a satisfying experience. Hard to say why. Maybe it was just a young boy's game to pass the time, like counting seams in the sidewalk. But maybe there was more to it than that.

Maybe it was the longing every young boy has.

The longing to be more to his dad than a child.

To be buddies.

On those walks together, my dad told me stories. Stories of his childhood. Stories of his days as a coach. Stories of the war.

War had always intrigued me, and I hung on to every word of those stories. As a child of the fifties, I grew up on images of war that were shaped by television and toy makers, images that fed a childhood craving for heroes and adventures. In the neighborhood I grew up in, the kids all played "Big Army" and "Little Army." For Big Army we were the soldiers. All the boys divided up sides, hiding in hedges, behind trees, in makeshift foxholes. We did all our own stunts, sprawling to the ground when wounded. And we did all our own sound effects, from machine-gun fire to grenades going off to incoming mortars whistling from the sky and exploding all around us.

Little Army was played with plastic army men. We'd build forts and tunnels and camouflaged machine-gun nests. The wounds inflicted on our army men were brushed with red nail polish. And no matter how bloodied, they survived, always against insurmountable odds, to fight again, taking the hill held by the enemy, freeing the prisoners, and coming home as heroes.

Only in war—real war—the soldiers weren't all heroes.

And they didn't all come home.

I didn't know that, though, until my dad told me *his* stories. Stories about how he lived and what he ate.

What combat was like. And what it was like to liberate a concentration camp. I remember those stories to this day.

The stories about his childhood, though, were my favorite.

Stories about the neighborhood he grew up in and the games the kids played: "Go-sheepy-go" and "Kick the can."

Stories about his mother, who died when he was four, and about how good a person she was and how hard she worked. Her week was divided into distinct segments, like seven generous slices from a loaf of homemade bread. Monday was washday. Sunday was church. The days in between were reserved for things like cleaning house, baking, taking baths.

Stories about home remedies and Halloween pranks. Stories about his dad…who he was…what he did…why my dad loved him so much…what he missed about his dad once he was gone.

Stories about his first date and the summers between his high-school years when he went to Chicago to work in the steel mills, shoveling coal into great open-hearth furnaces.

That's how we passed the time, with stories. Dad was the storyteller. I was the listener. A perfect match for an evening walk.

Growing up, I dreamed about being an oceanographer or a forest ranger.

I ended up a writer. A teller of stories.

Who knows how my life would have turned out, in a thousand ways but at least vocationally, if my dad hadn't had that heart attack during my formative years. What if it had come when I was in college? What if we had not taken those long walks together, those endless walks down those lamplit streets that lengthened the stride of my imagination?

The stories my dad told mingled with the firefly evenings in a magical way. They conveyed to me a sense of place, a sense of time, and somehow a sense of the sacredness of life. They aroused in me a curiosity about the past, and with it, a sense that my life had roots, that my story was an extension of some older story whose origins went back for generations. I sensed somehow that it was an ongoing story as well. One that was being passed on to me. One that I would pass on someday myself.

Someday I would have children of my own. And stories to tell them. *My* stories. Stories that would fill them with a sense of curiosity…and adventure…and a sense of rootedness.

Sacred stories.

Stories that stretch across the generations like a bridge.

And as the generations come together through the stories they share, we will see, maybe for the first time, that God is not only in the bridge, He is the One who has been building it all along.

❧

Remember the former things long past,
For I am God, and there is no other;
I am God, and there is no one like Me,
Declaring the end from the beginning
And from ancient times things which have not been done,
Saying, "My purpose will be established,
And I will accomplish all My good pleasure."

ISAIAH 46:9-10

You are told a lot about your education,

but some beautiful, sacred memory,

preserved since childhood,

is perhaps the best education of all.

FYODOR DOSTOEVSKY

~

Sources

"Thanks for Teaching Me the Value of Faith" adapted from
In My Father's House: The years before "The Hiding Place"
by Corrie ten Boom with C. C. Carlson, copyright
© 1976. Used by permission of Fleming H. Revell, a
division of Baker Book House Company.

"Thanks for Teaching Me the Value of God" adapted from
God of My Father by Dr. Larry Crabb, Jr. and Lawrence
Crabb, Sr. Copyright © 1994 by Lawrence J. Crabb, Jr.,
Ph.D., P.A., dba, Institute of Biblical Counseling and
Lawrence J. Crabb, Sr. Used by permission of Zondervan
Publishing House.

"Thanks for Teaching Me the Value of Me" adapted from
*Things We Wish We Had Said: Reflections of a Father and
His Grown Son* by Tony and Bart Campolo, copyright ©
1989, Word Publishing, Nashville, Tennessee. All rights
reserved.

"Thanks for Teaching Me the Value of Humility" adapted
from *Lessons from a Father to His Son* by John Ashcroft
with Gary Thomas, copyright © 1998. Used by permission of Thomas Nelson Publishers.

About the Author

KEN GIRE is a graduate of Texas Christian University and Dallas Theological Seminary. He is the award-winning author of more than a dozen books, including *Moments with the Savior, Windows of the Soul,* and *The Reflective Life.* A full-time writer, he resides with his wife, Judy, in Monument, Colorado, and is the proud father of four pretty terrific children.

Ally

Brandon Cell   Omar
232 3642   910 - 74
             474 6703